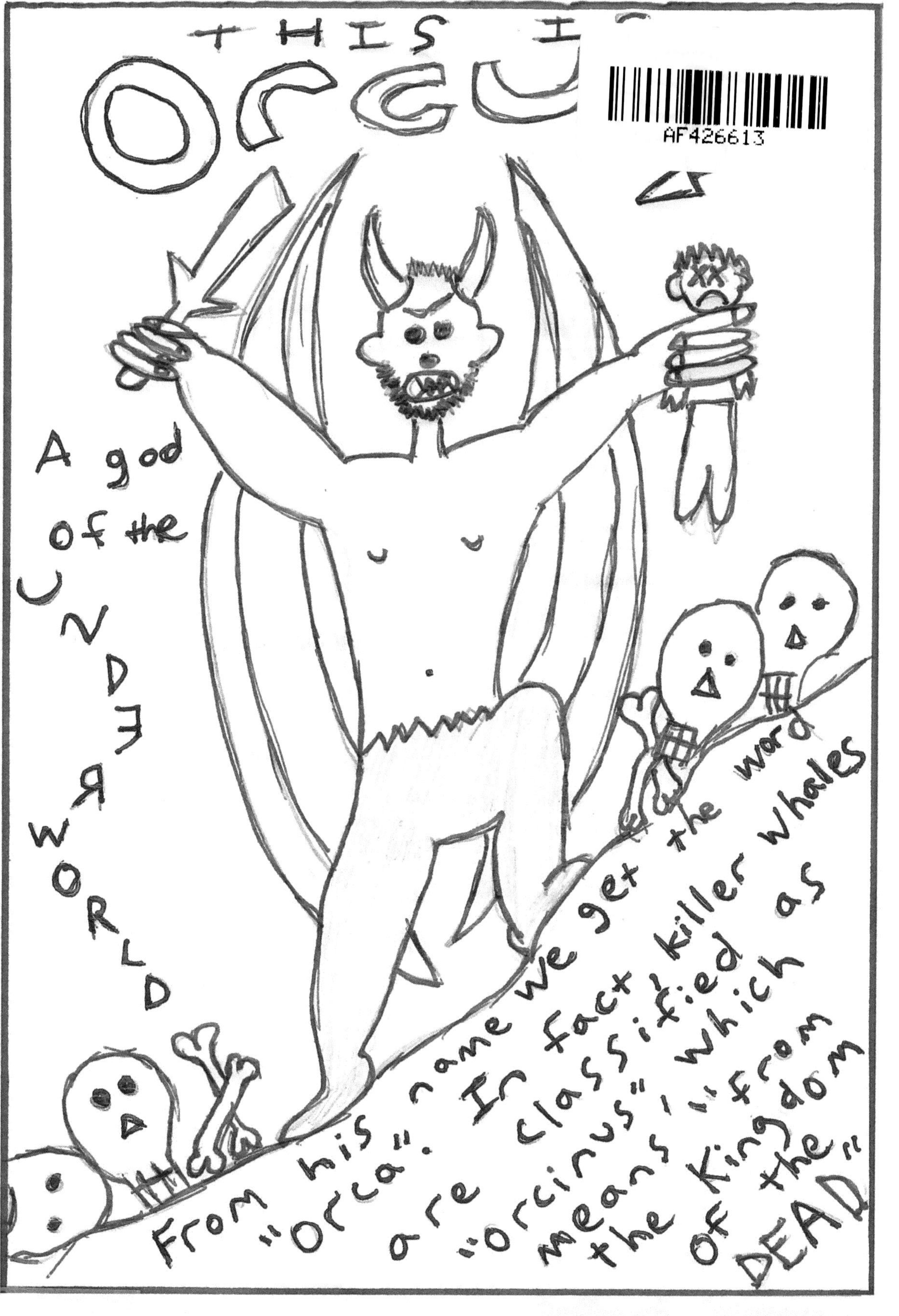

THIS ORCU
AF426613
A god of the UNDERWORLD
From his name we get the word "Orca". In fact killer whales are classified as "orcinus" which means "from the Kingdom of the DEAD"

When I was four years old, my parents took me to Seaworld.
SHAMU
Are you ready to see Shamu the killer whale?
Shamu the what?!
Maybe you'll get to ride on his back!
WHAT?!

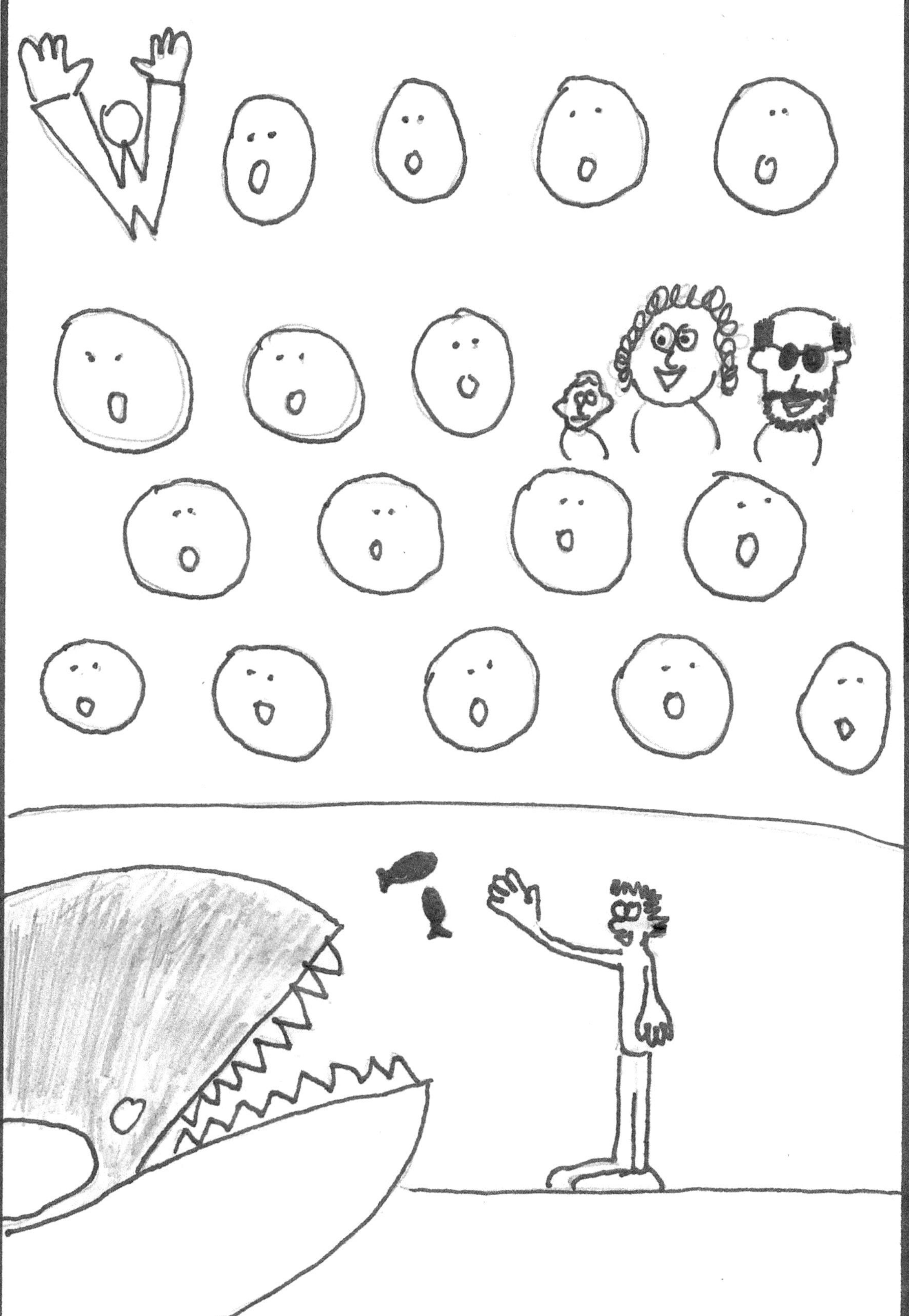

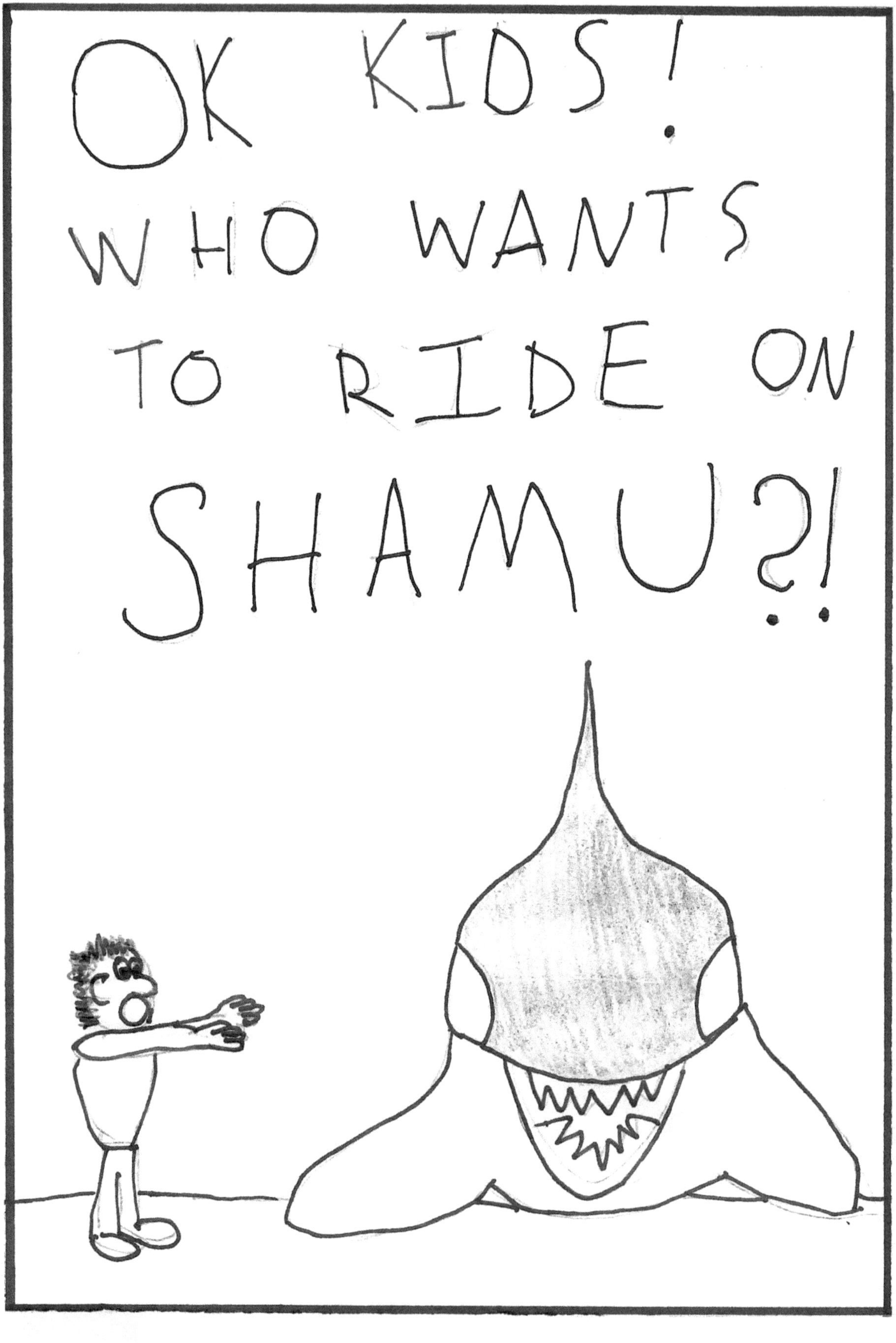

OK KIDS!
WHO WANTS
TO RIDE ON
SHAMU?!

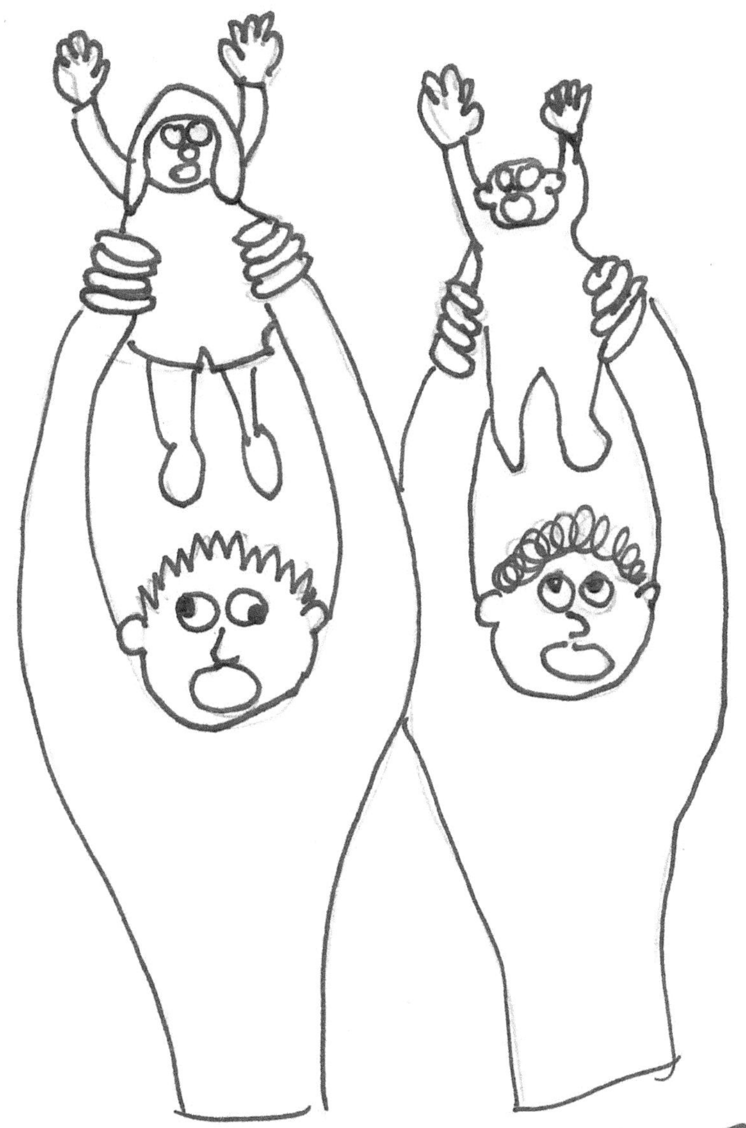

Thunder erupted from every parent and child in the stadium.

Except for me.
I did not want to
go near that thing.

But they picked me anyway.

My mom
did a
backflip.

I was taken from the safety of my seat and led to a mouthful of teeth, glistening in the Florida sun.

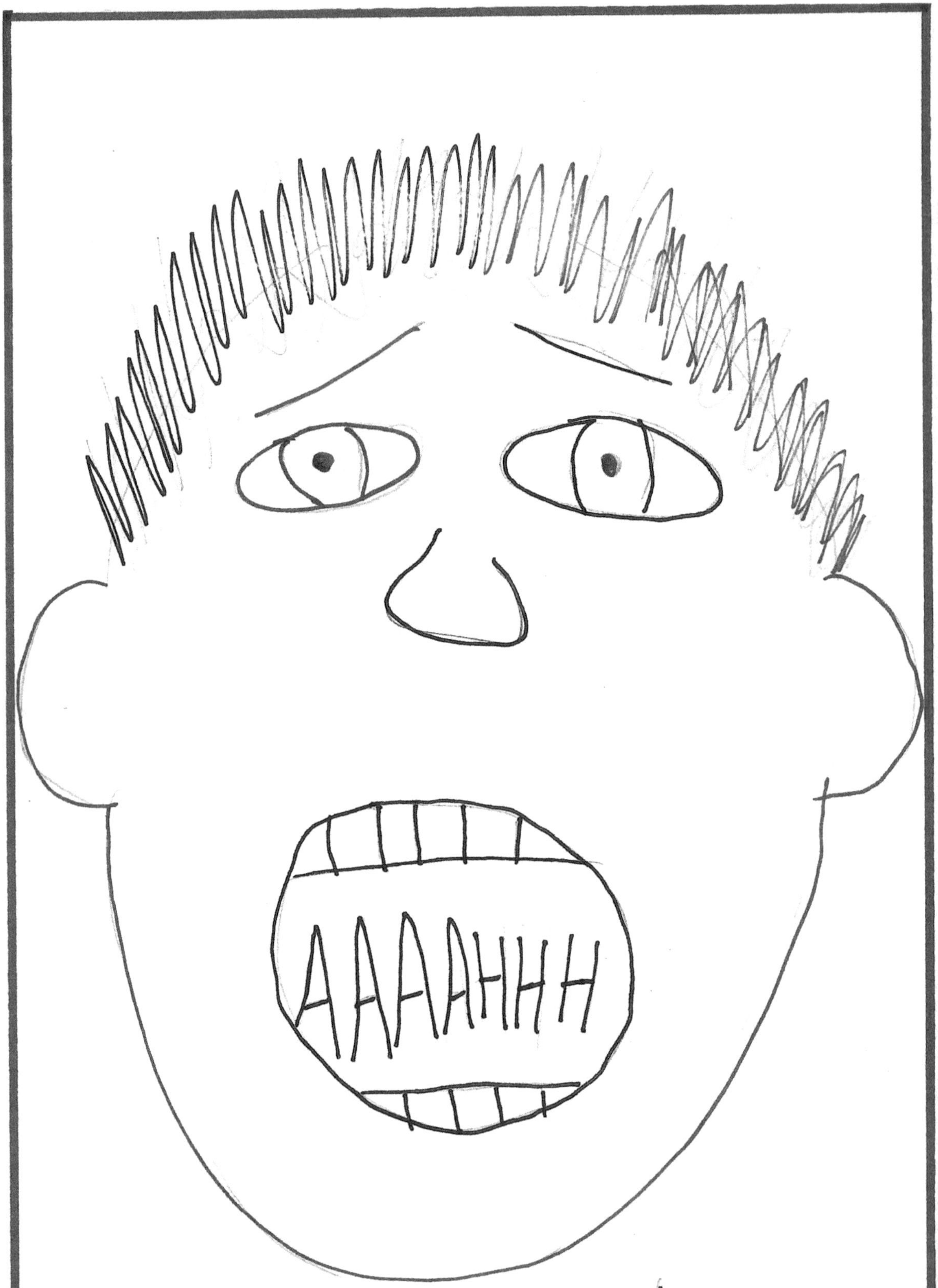

I politely declined.

What's wrong? Don't you know how hard I prayed to God for you to be chosen?

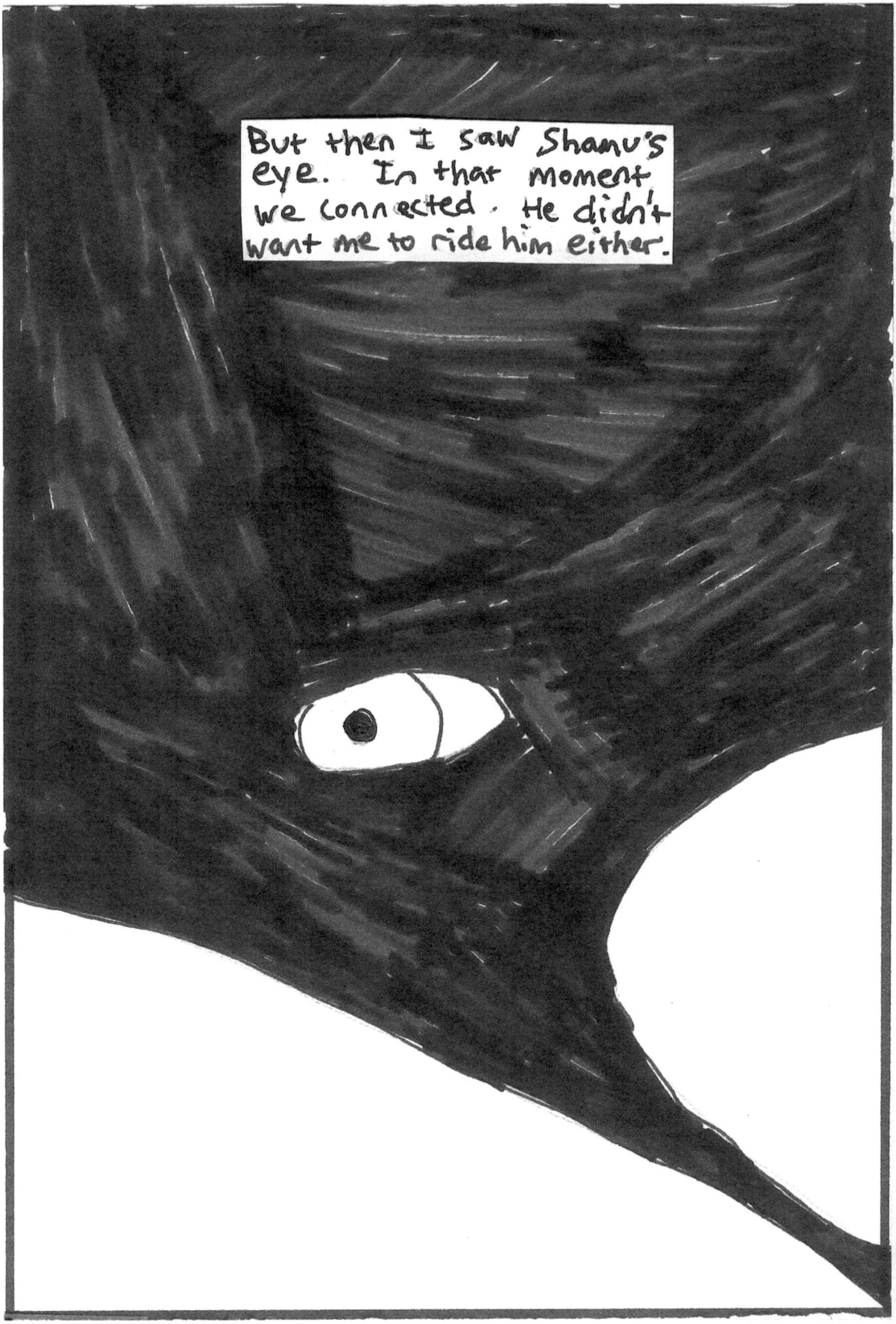

But then I saw Shamu's eye. In that moment we connected. He didn't want me to ride him either.

My fear left me.
The longer
I looked
into his
eye...

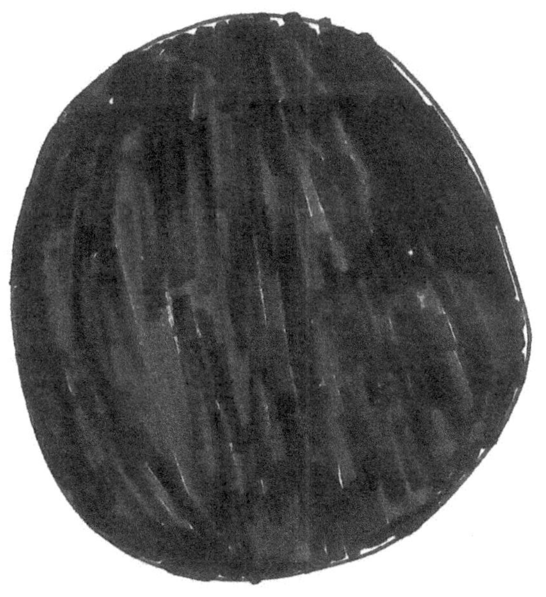

... the better I felt.

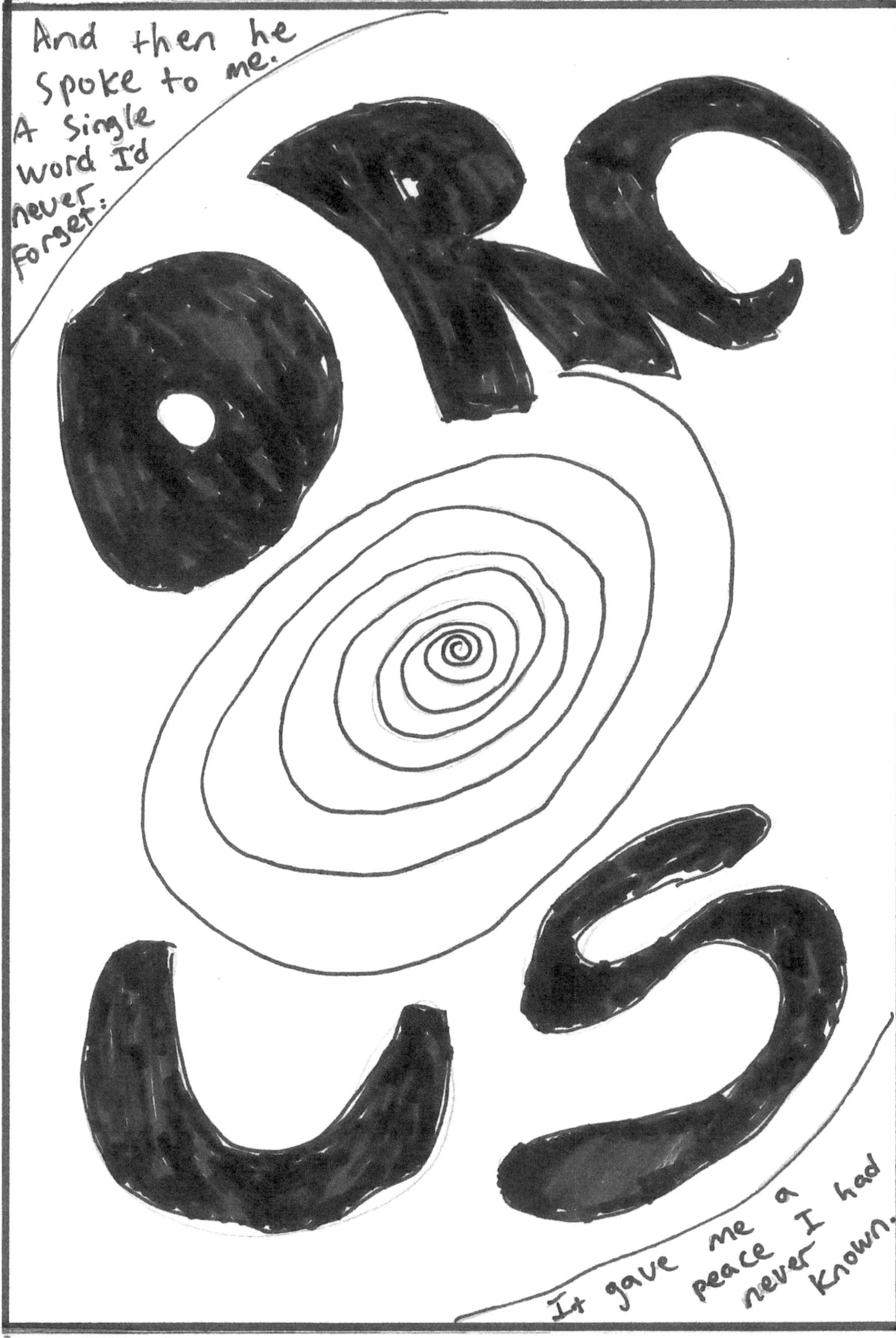

And then he spoke to me. A single word I'd never forget:
ORCUS
It gave me a peace I had never known.

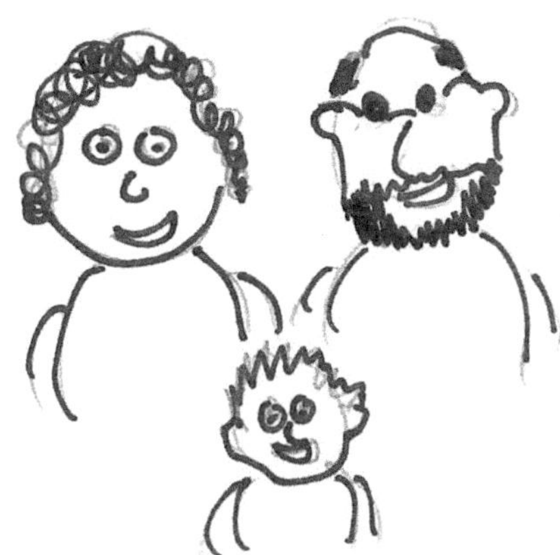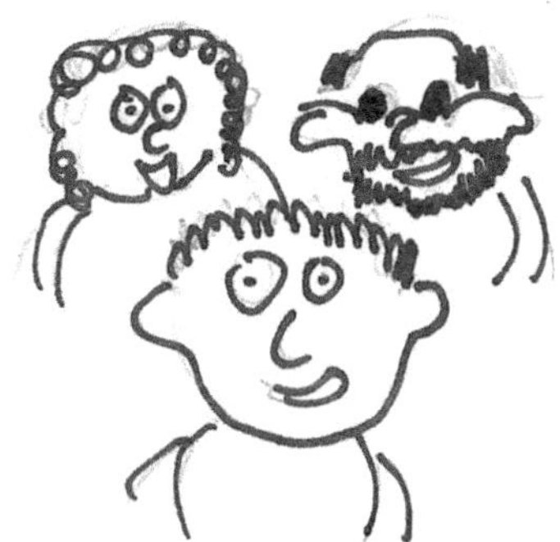

Years passed.

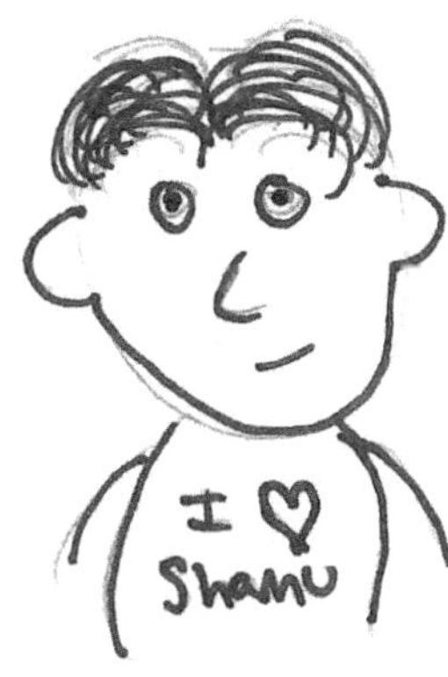

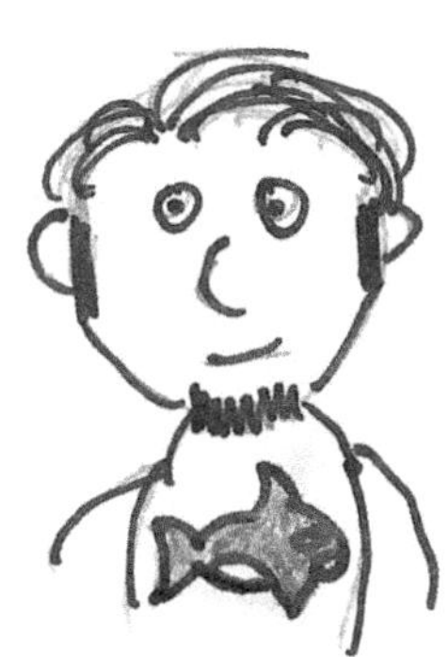

I obsessed over reconnecting with Orcus.

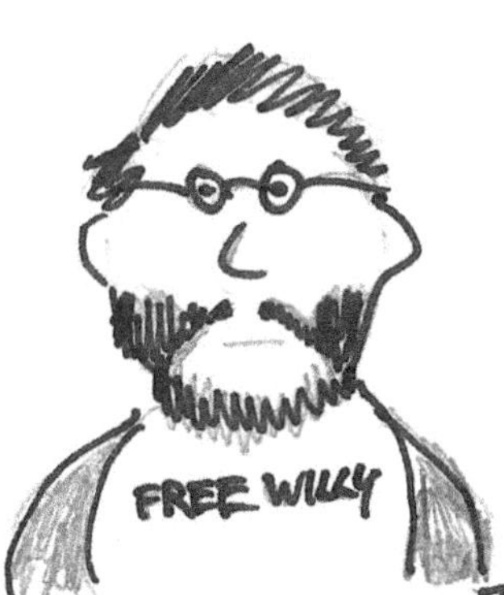

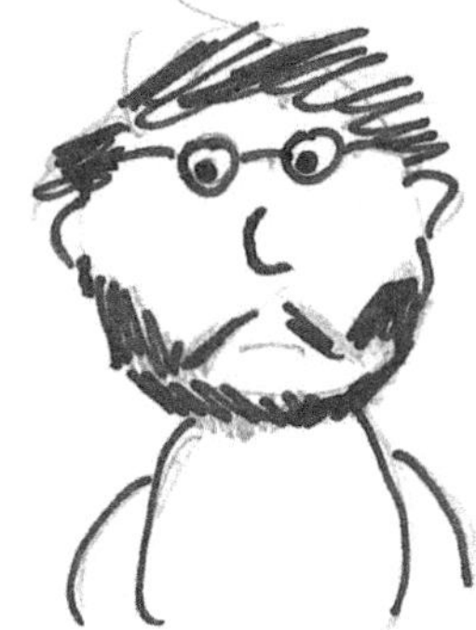

It became a lifestyle nobody could understand.

I couldn't keep a job.

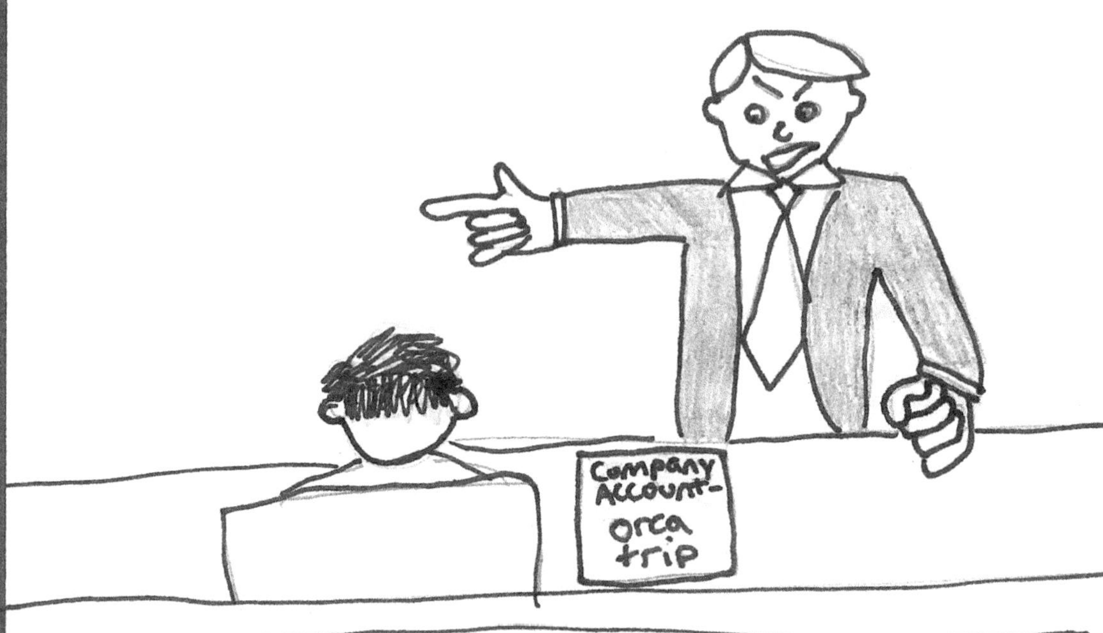

Company
Account—
Orca
trip

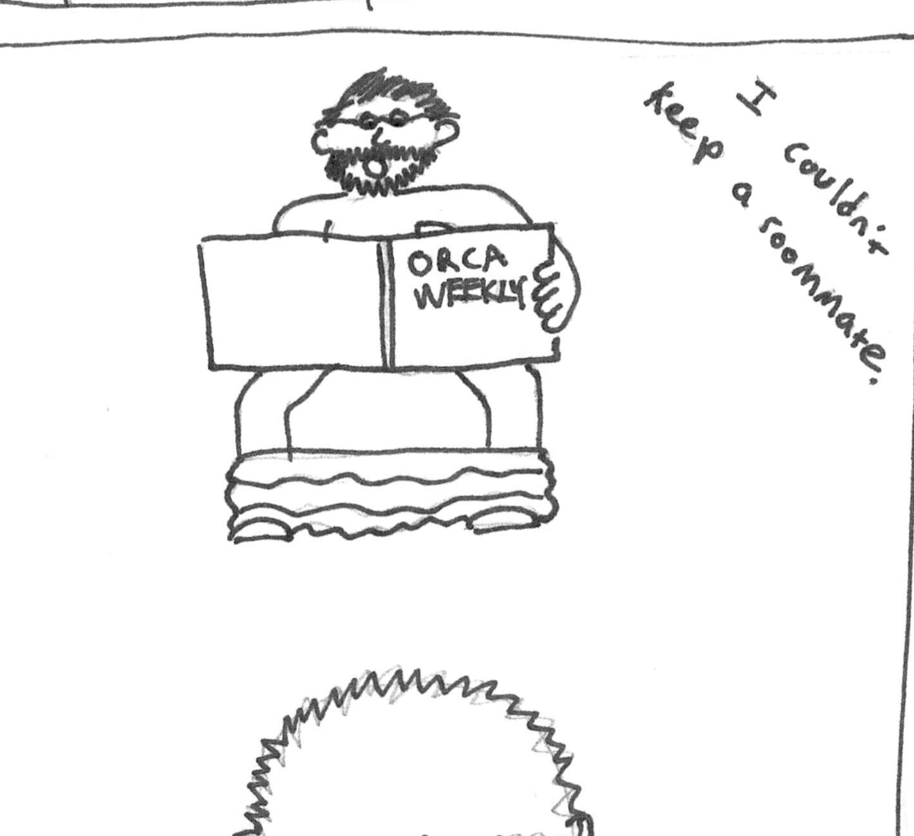

ORCA
WEEKLY
I couldn't keep a roommate.

After awhile, I couldn't even leave the water.

But Orcus never came.

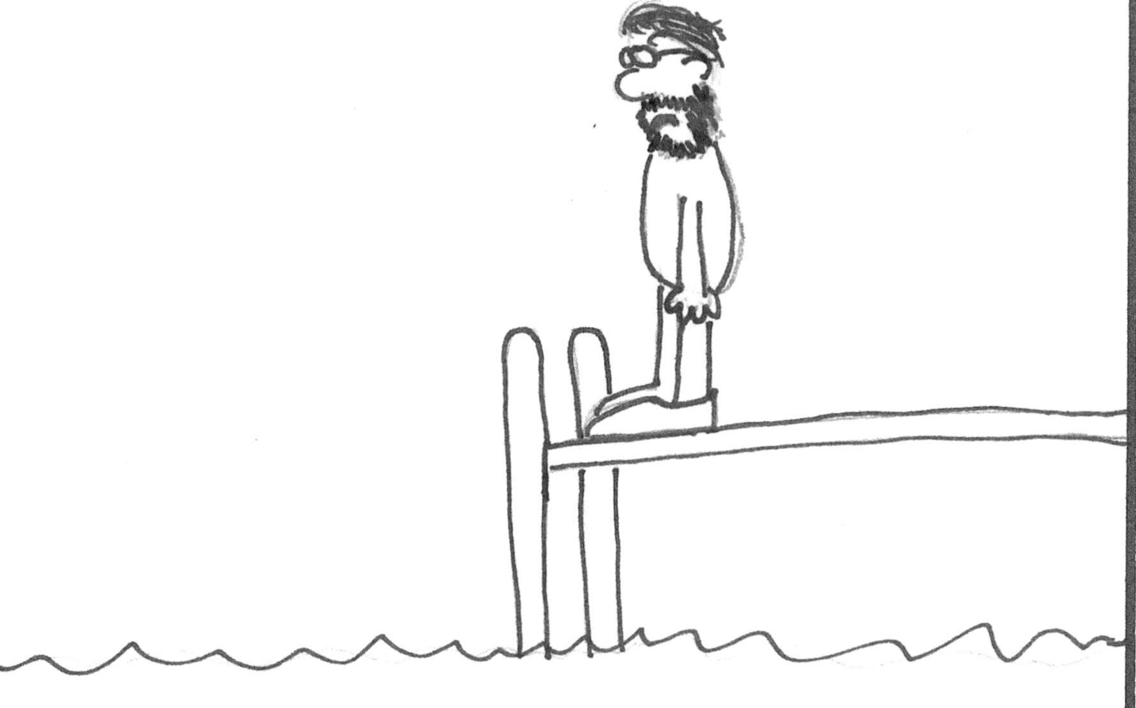

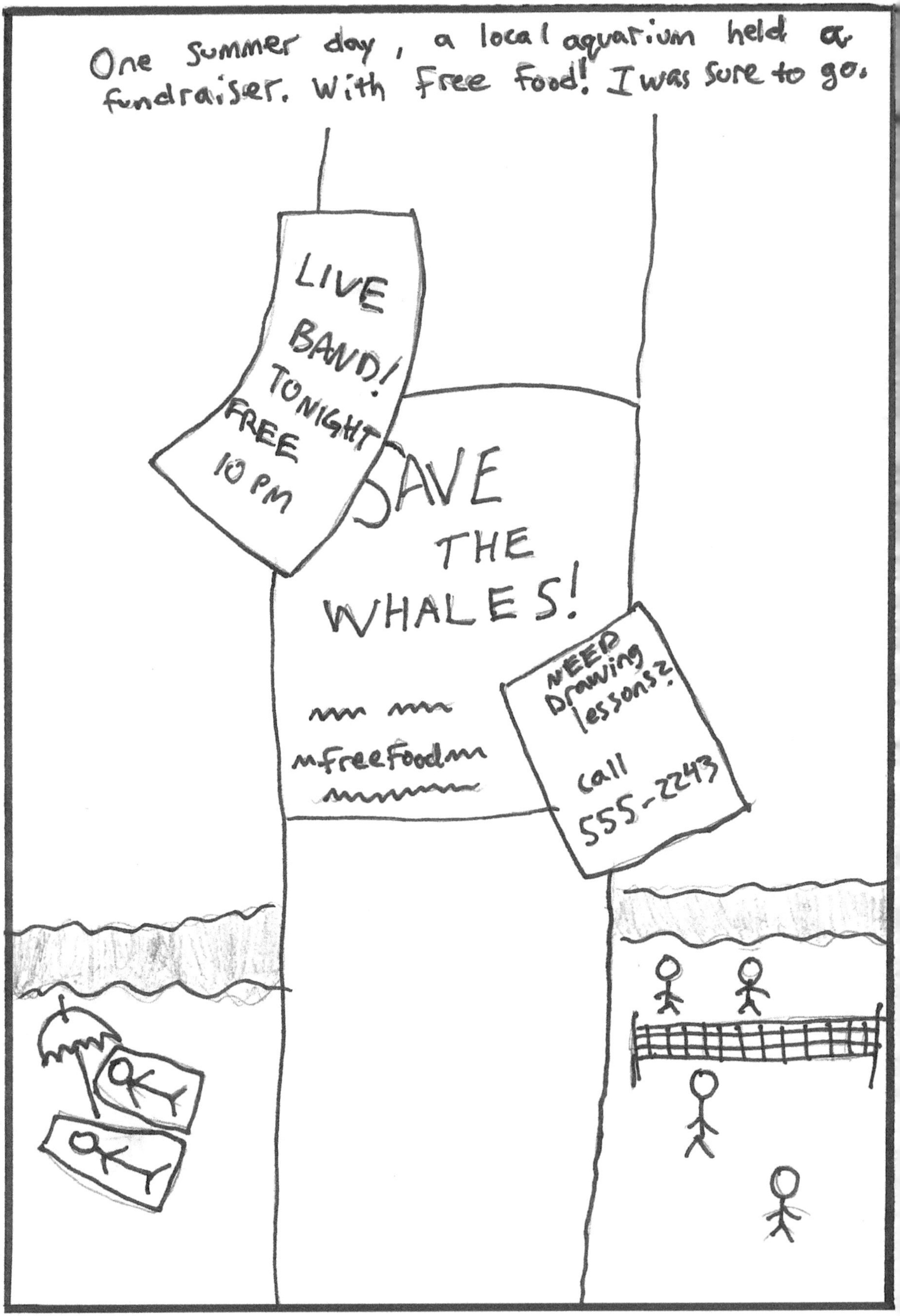

One summer day, a local aquarium held a fundraiser. With free food! I was sure to go.
LIVE BAND! TONIGHT FREE 10 PM
SAVE THE WHALES!
Free Food
NEED Drawing lessons? call 555-2243

I never made it to the buffet.

Displayed in the lobby was a
life-sized model orca.

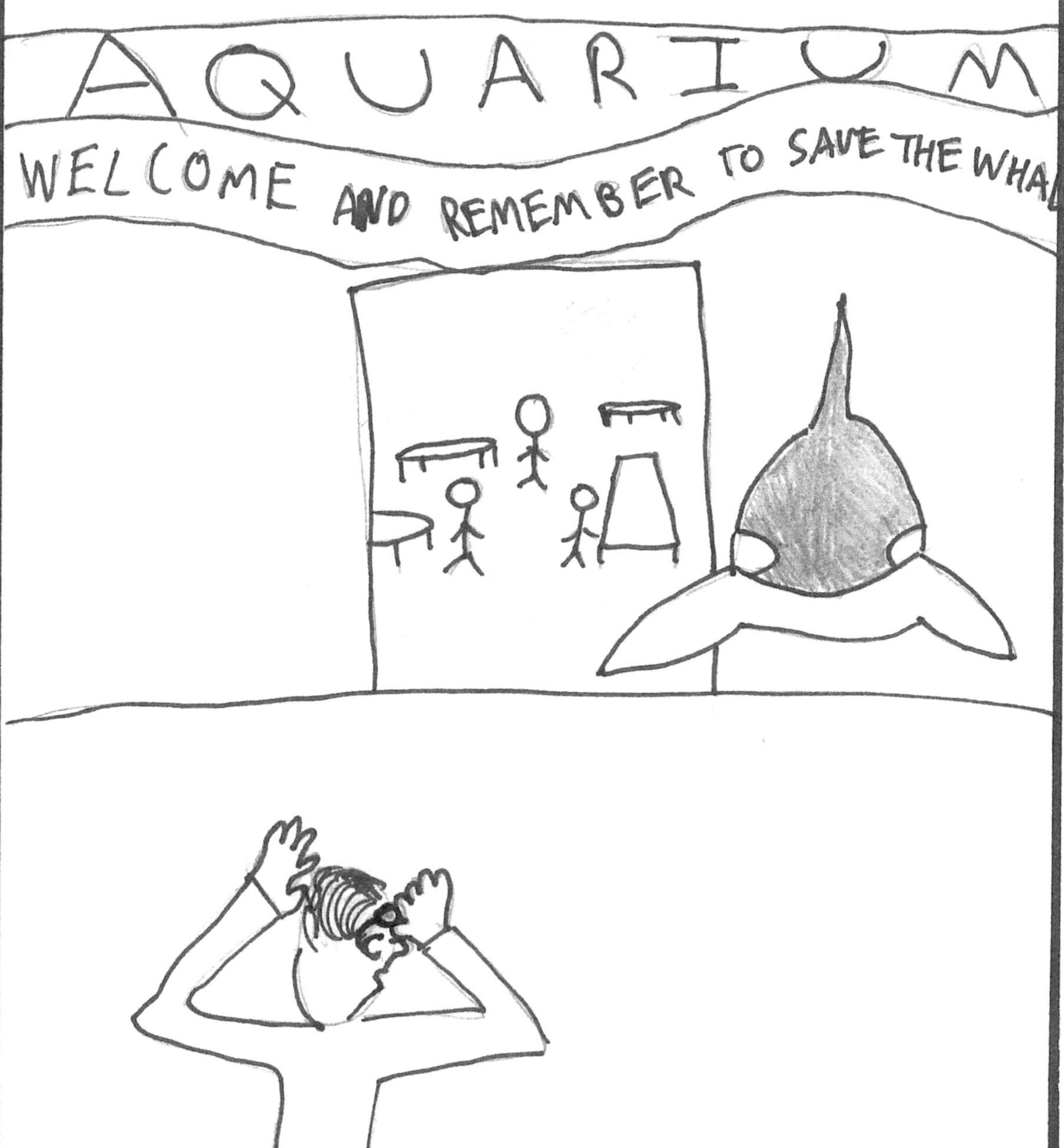

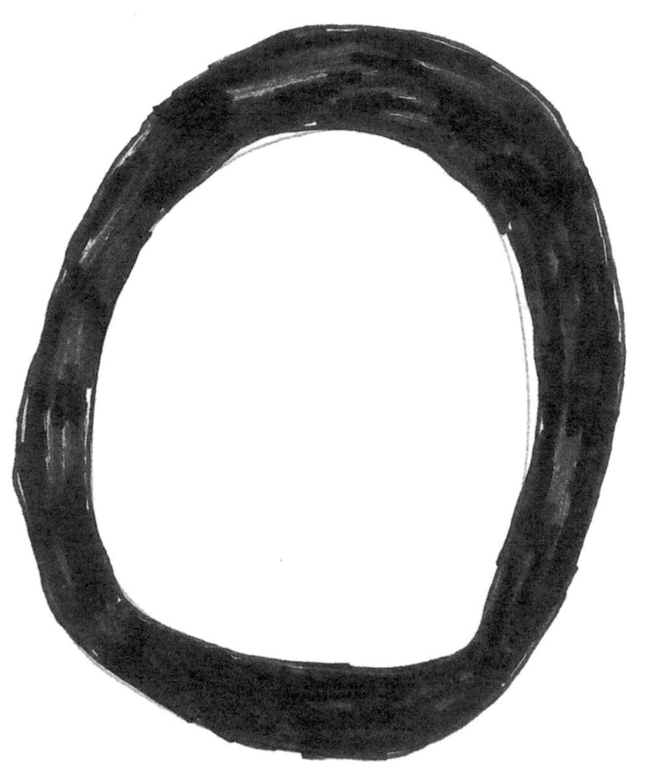

I stared into
the marble eye.

It said nothing.

Was I losing it?

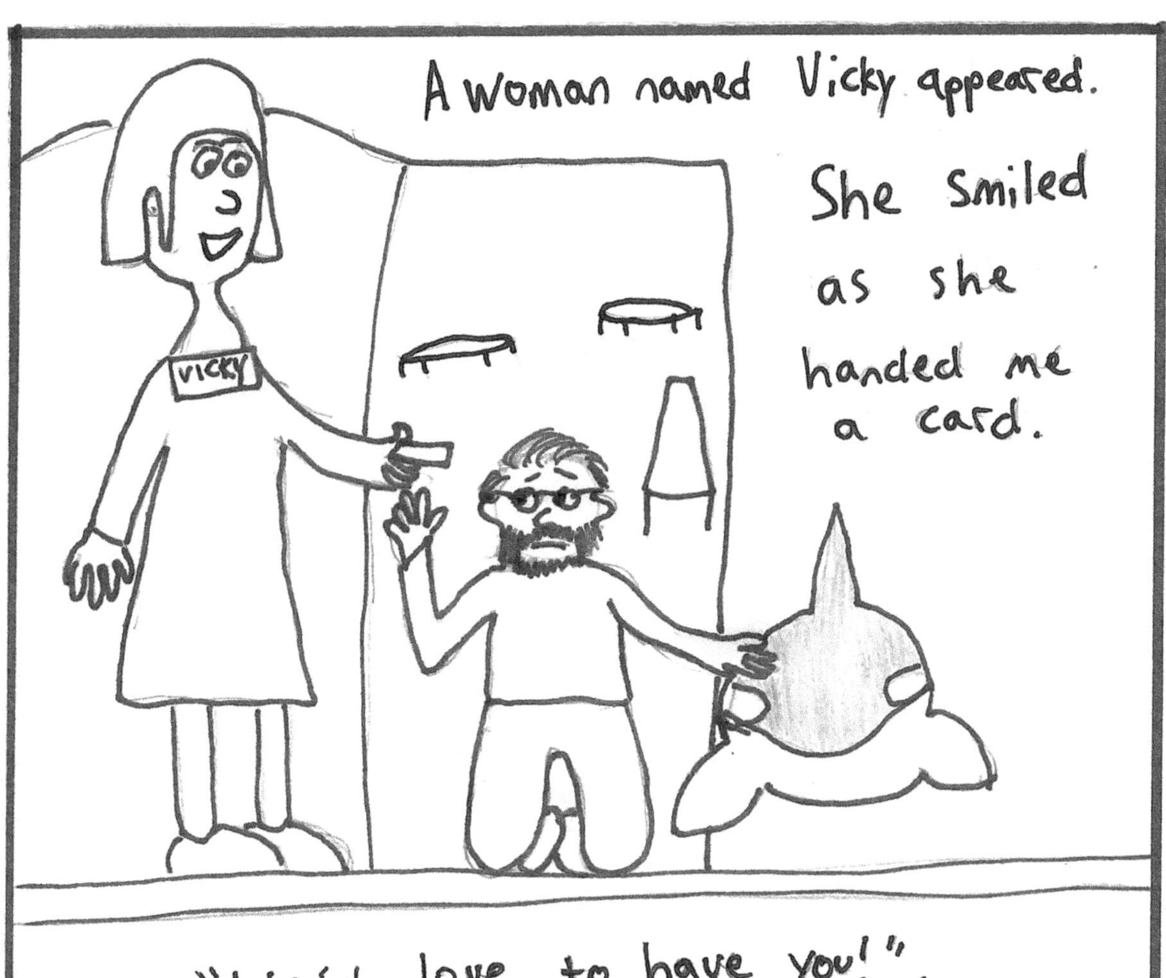

"We'd love to have you!",
she said.

The Church of Orcus
Join us!
Thursdays at midnight
(address on back)

My jaw dropped.

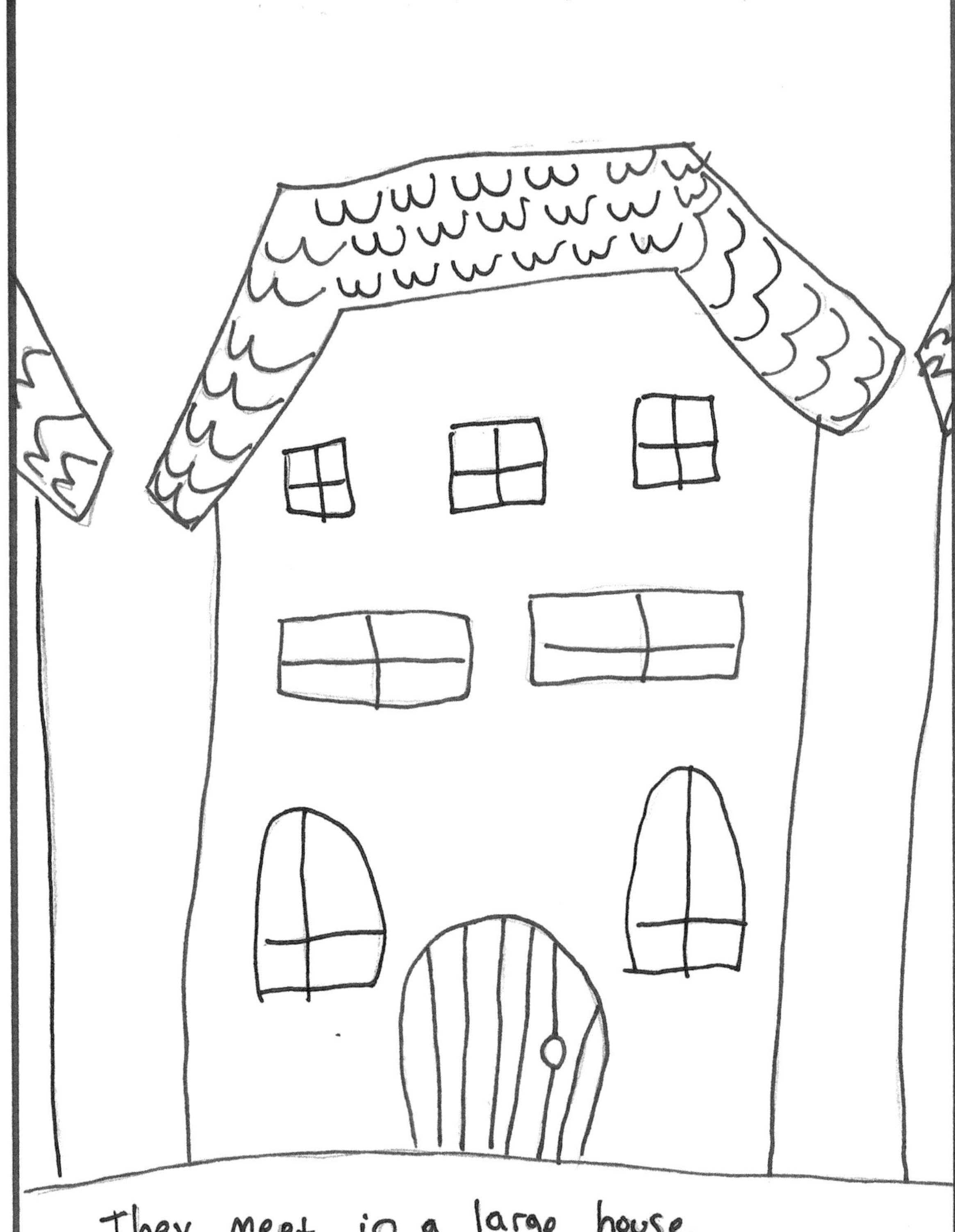

They meet in a large house
in the middle of the night.

They have an indoor pool, deeper and larger than any pool I've ever seen.

Swimming in the pool is a massive orca, said to be thousands of years old. They call him
ORCUS.

He surfaced and looked right at me. I fell to the ground as I felt myself get lost in the hypnotic stare of his eye

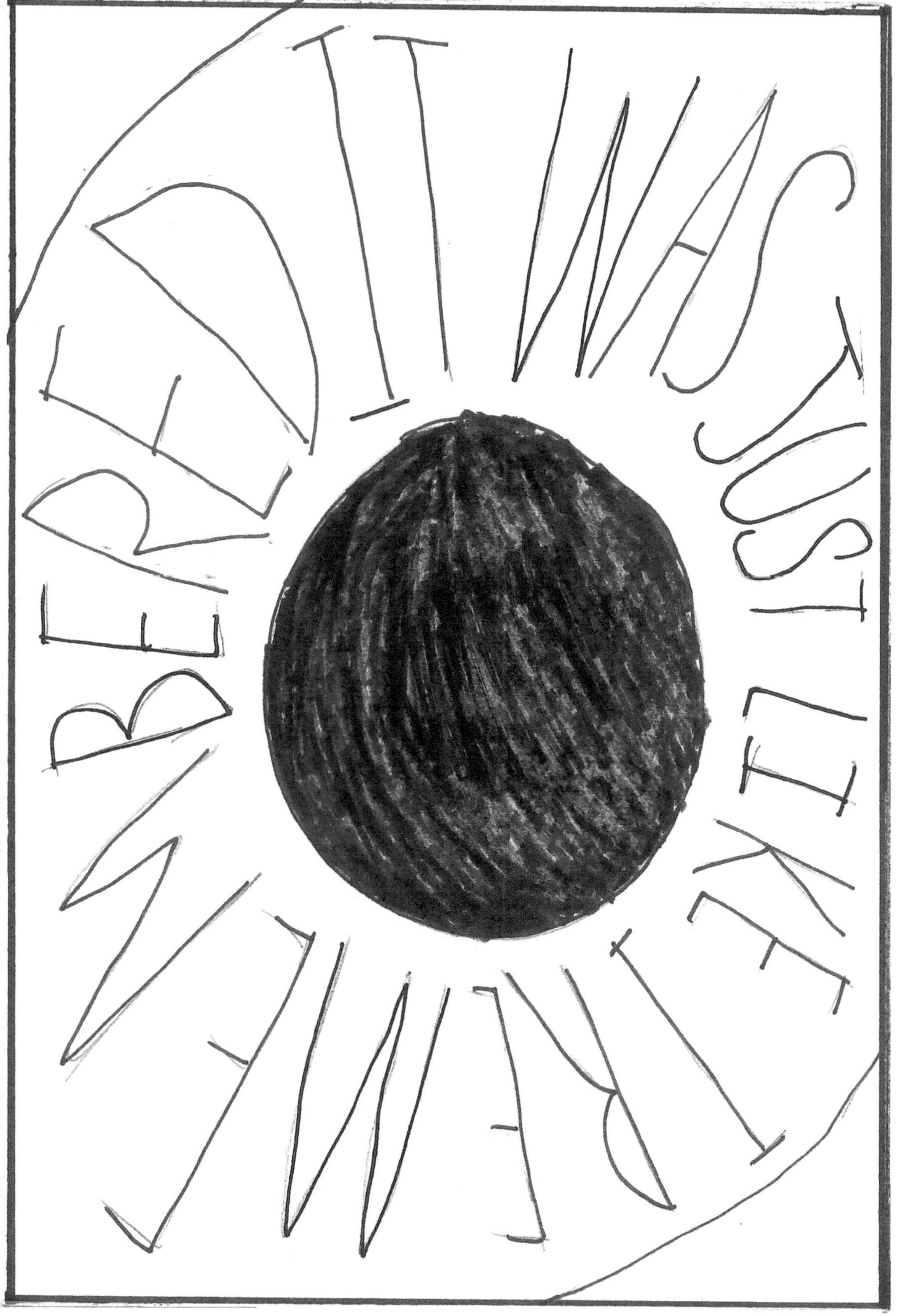
REMEMBERED IT WAS JUST LIKE IT WAS WHEN

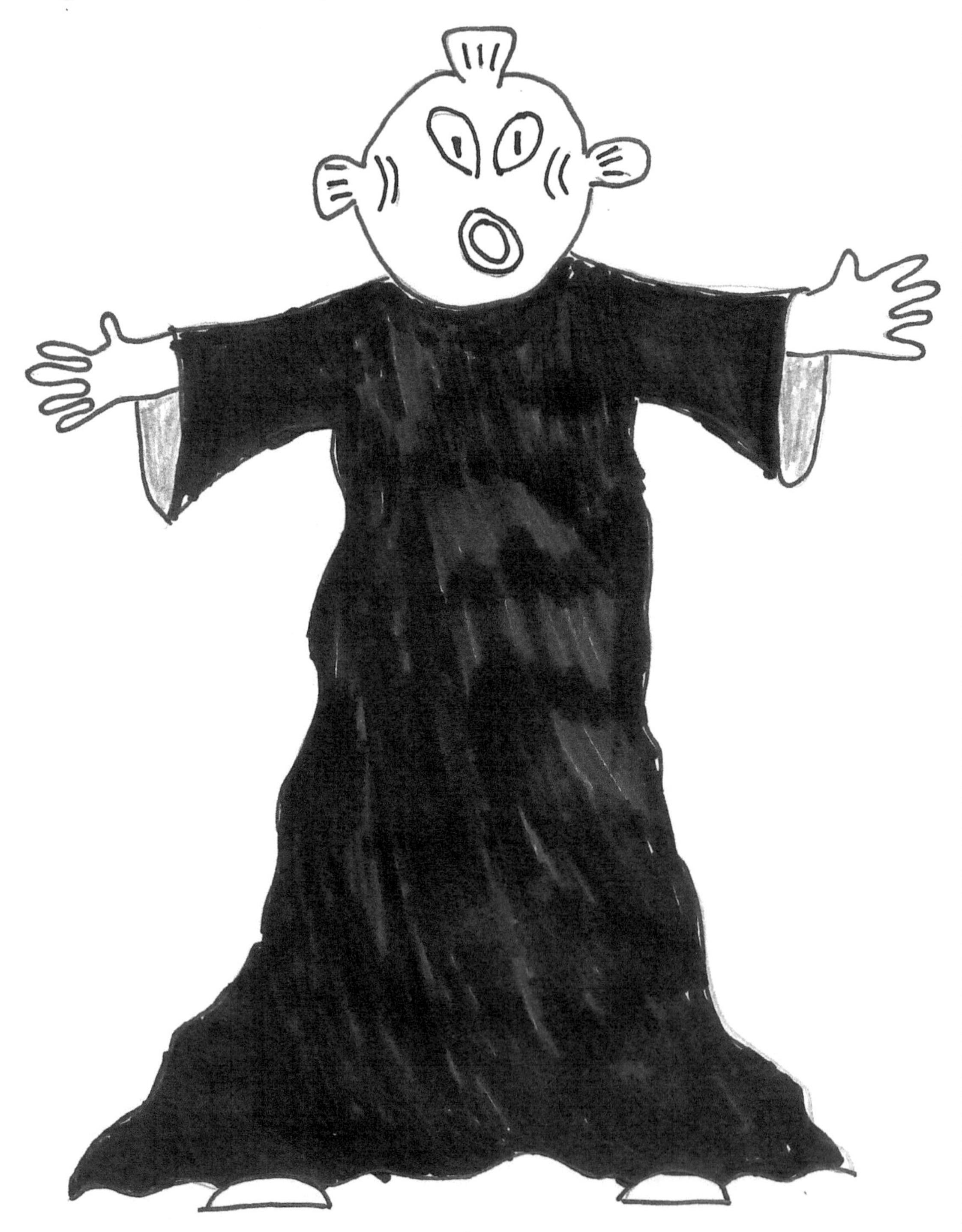
A priest in a wooden fish mask
said a prayer in an ancient language.

Vicky led a man to the water using a rope tied around his neck. His head was covered by a burlap sack.

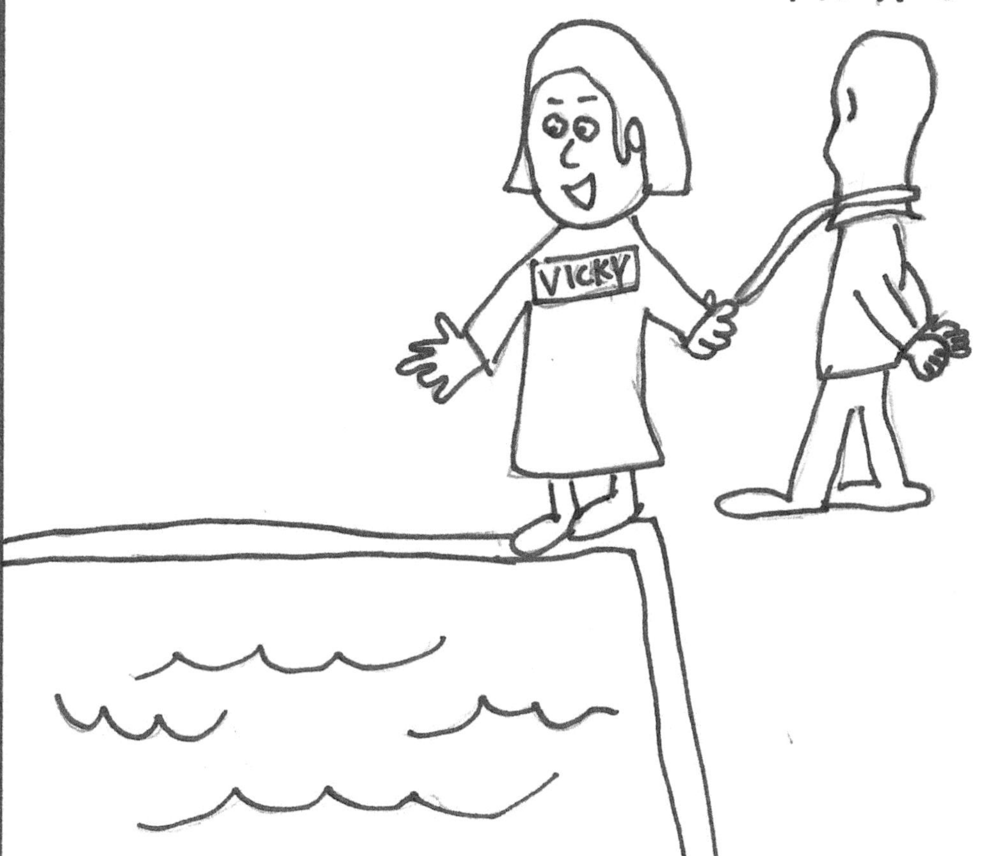

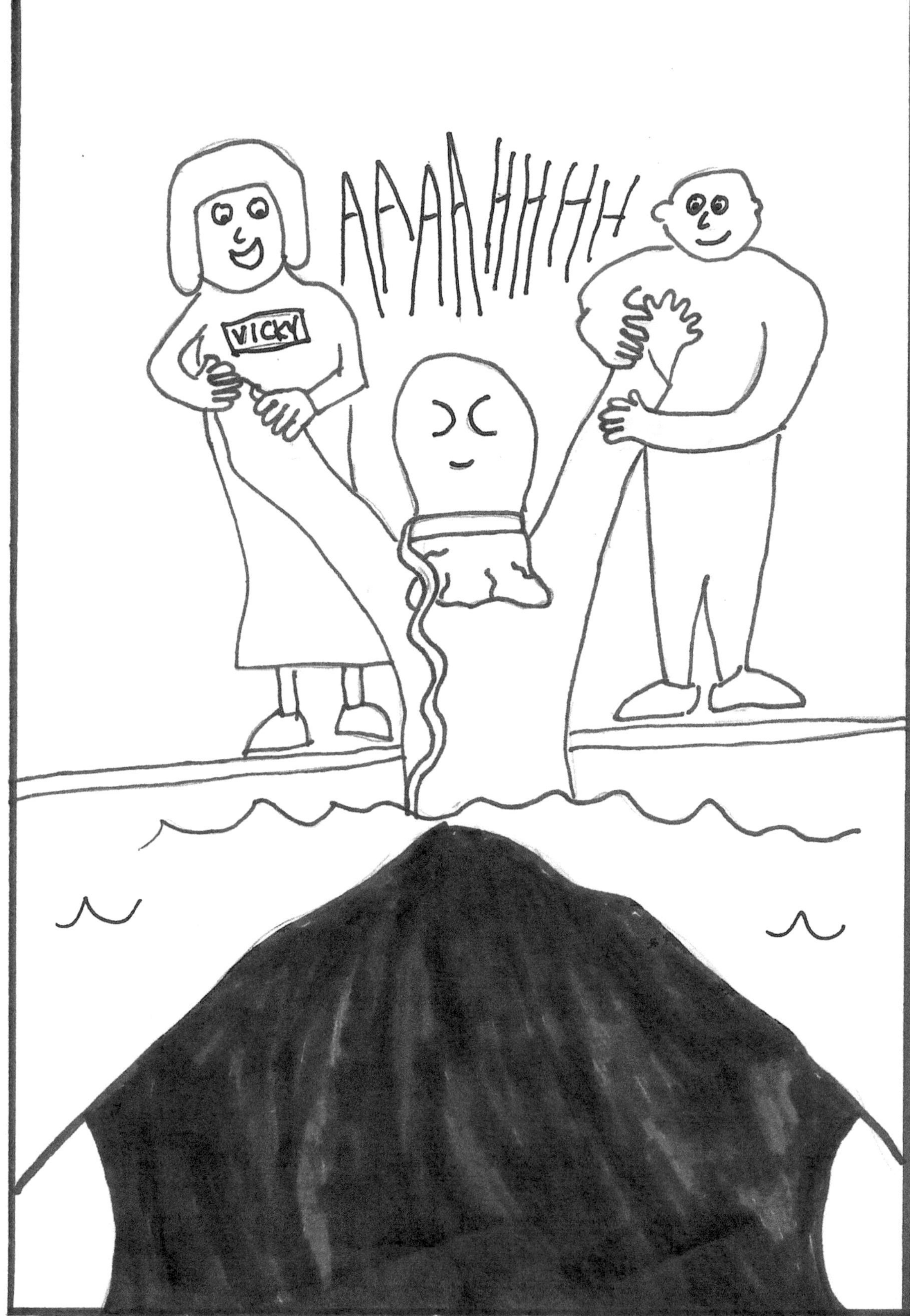

VICKY
AAAAHHHHH

I watched as everybody started
their dinner. This was normal for them.

Soon they finished. I still hadn't taken a bite. They started to notice.

Silence suffocated the room.

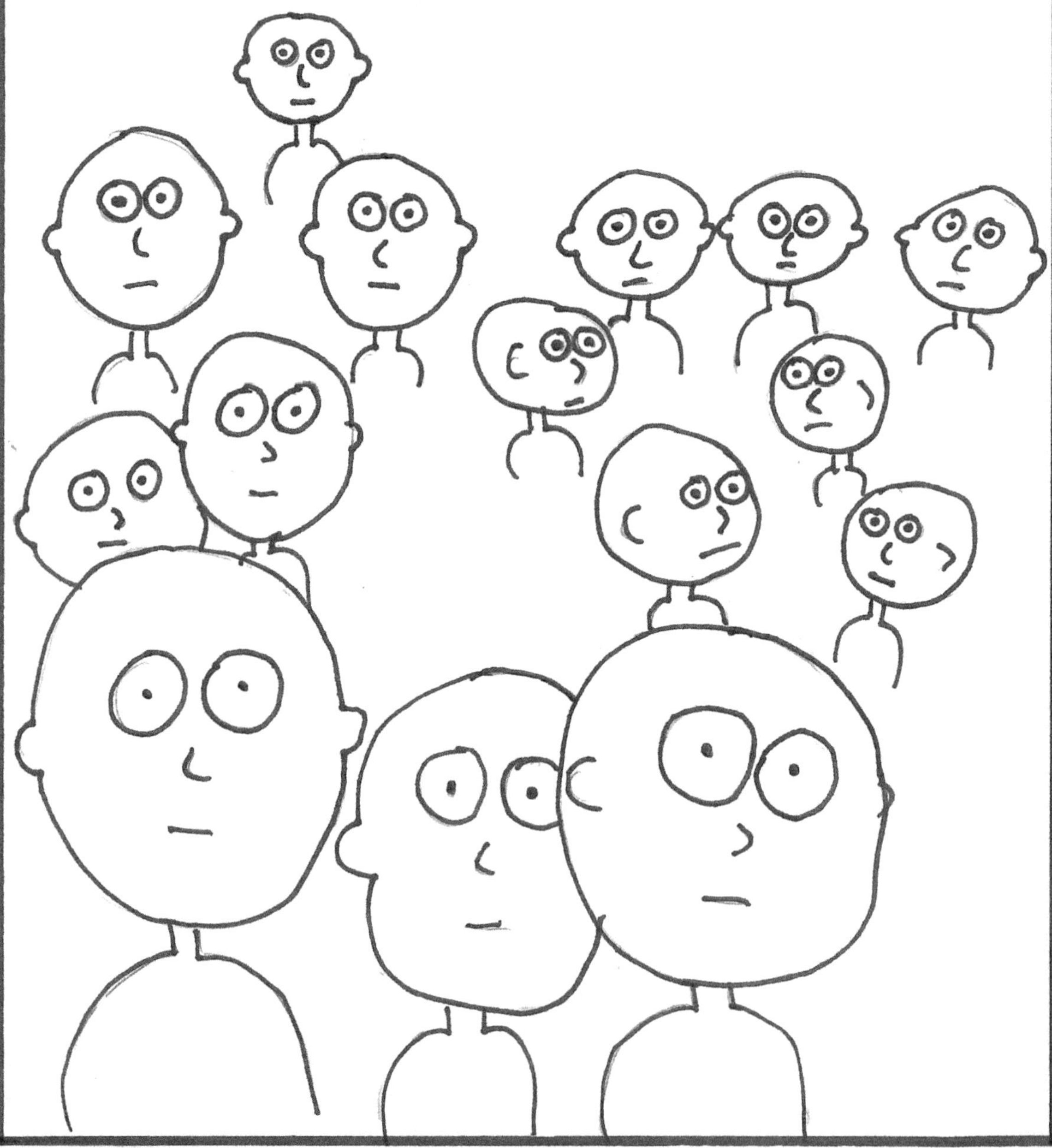

Vicky stepped forward.

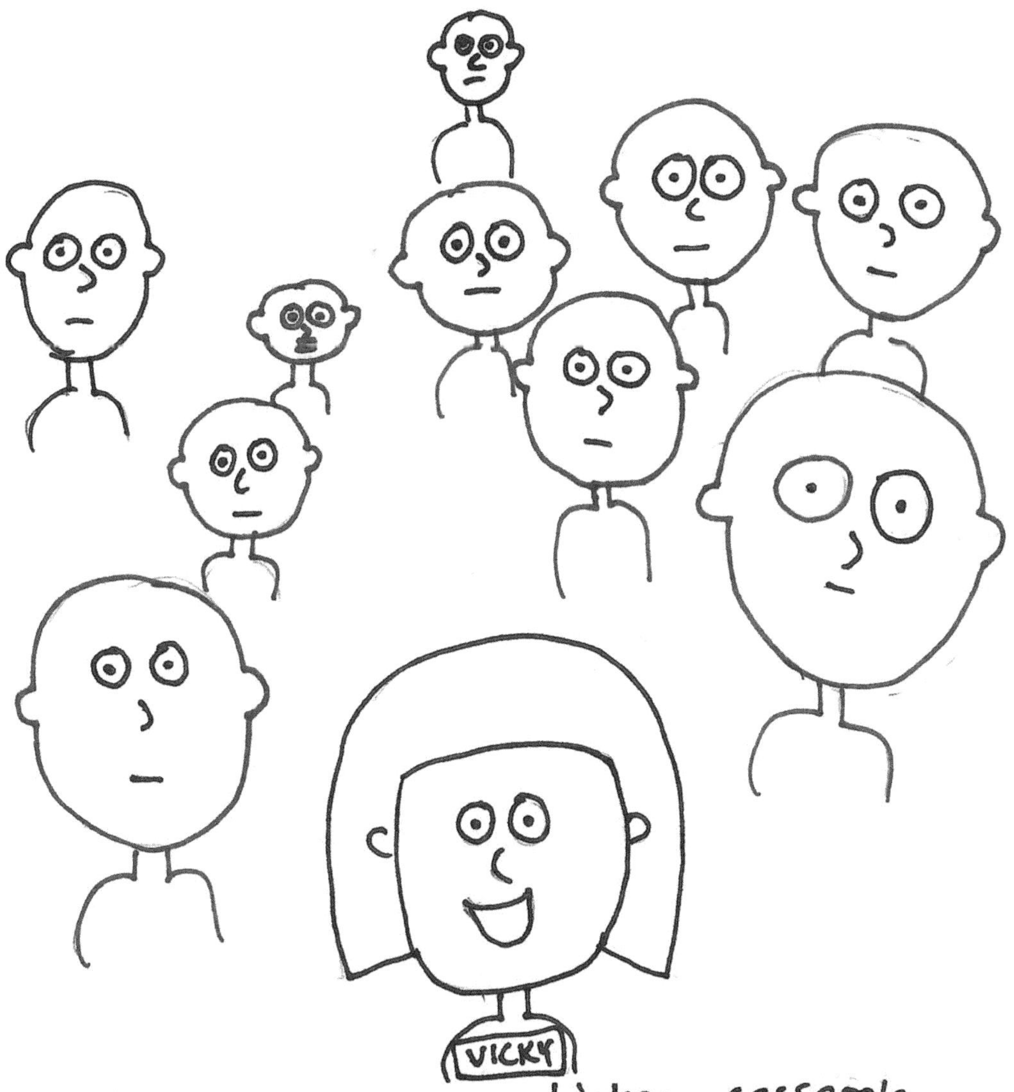

I made that chicken casserole.
Do you like it?

I took a bite.

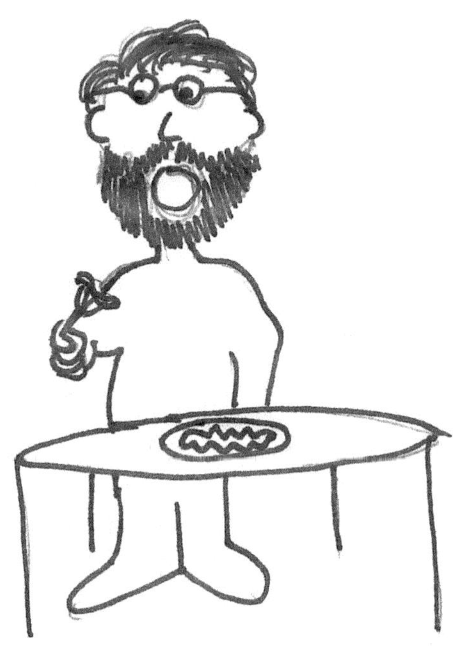

It was delicious.

A few months
have passed.
One day while
on a walk in
a park, I
stumbled across
a man in a booth.

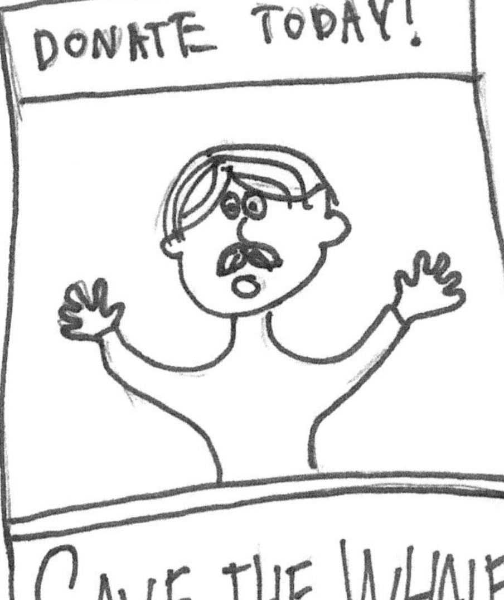

Excuse me can I get a minute of your time? this won't take long I promise.

We're doing our part to make a difference!

Are you familiar with our organization?

We welcome one-time gifts too!

We'd love to talk to you about a monthly donation.

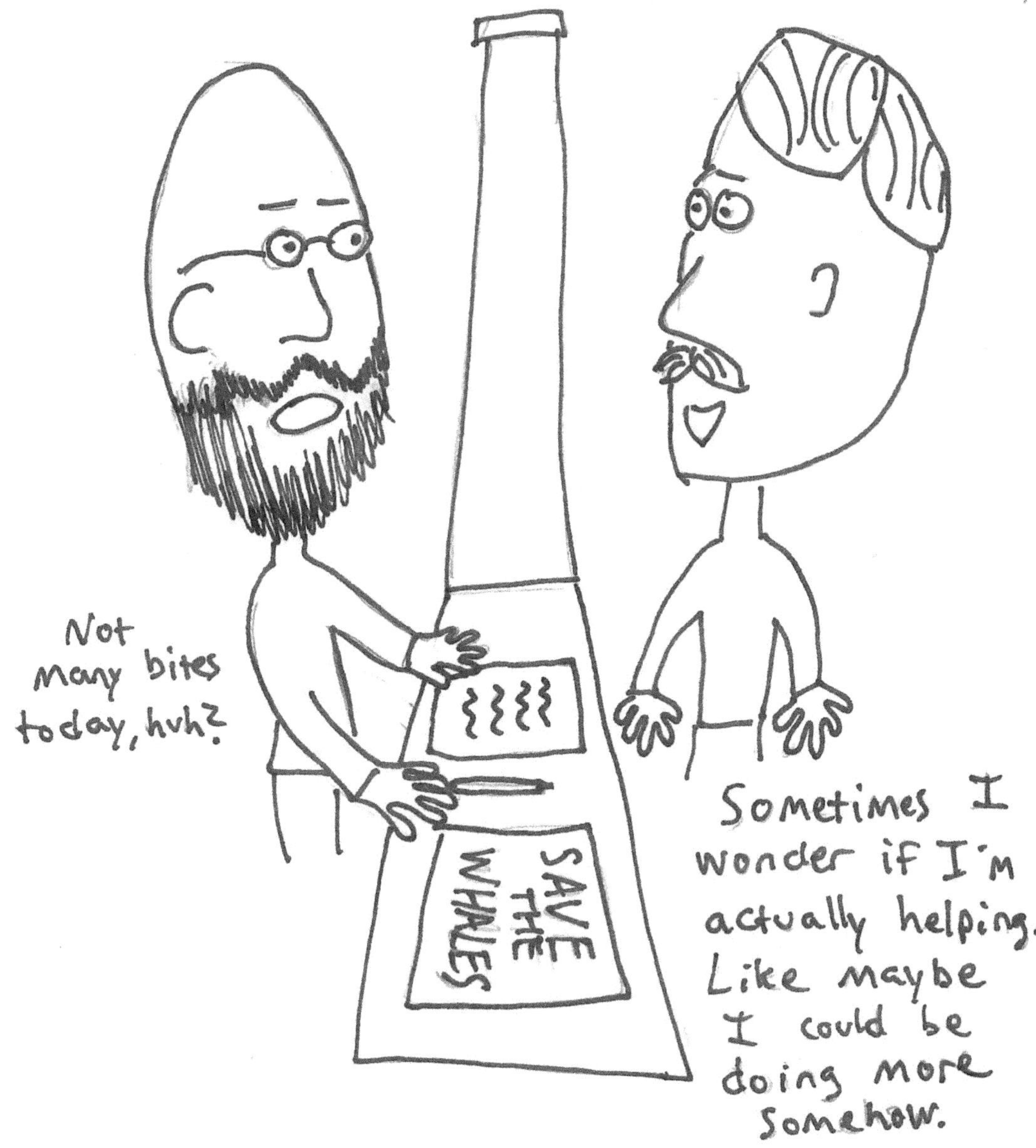

I'd like to donate.
Wow really? You're my first one!
Not many bites today, huh?
SAVE THE WHALES
Sometimes I wonder if I'm actually helping. Like maybe I could be doing more somehow.
I might know a way.

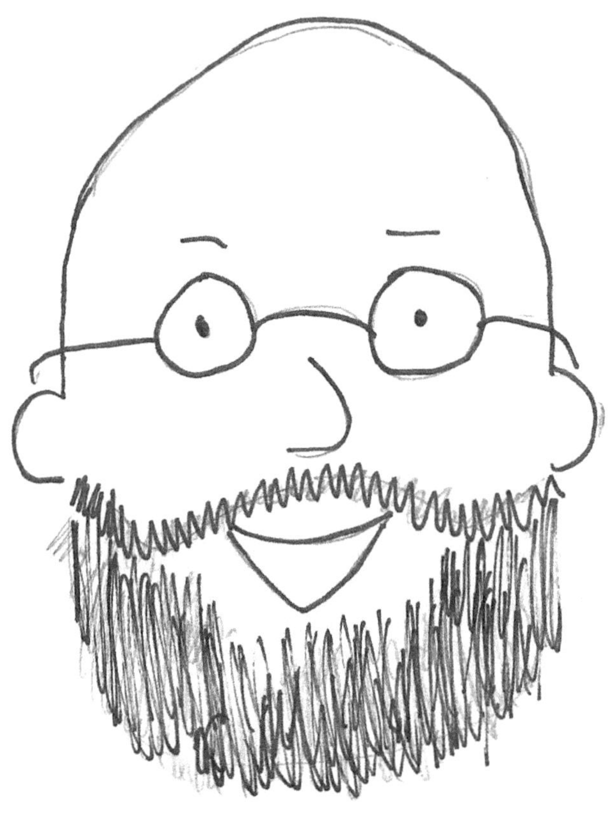

Do you like chicken casserole?

www.ingramcontent.com/pod-product-compliance
Lightning Source LLC
Chambersburg PA
CBHW041838110726
48006CB00020B/2670